To:

_____

From:

_____

For a Wonderful

Friend

new seasons™

A best friend willingly receives and carefully treasures the keys to your heart.

If life has introduced you to even one person you can call a true friend, you are truly blessed.

The miracle of friendship usually begins with a simple smile.

Building a friend-ship is like learning to dance. You take small, easy steps at first, then gradually add new ones until it becomes comfortable and familiar.

Value your friendship as your bank account; taking care to deposit more than you withdraw.

Good friends are like good windows—they let in the light and keep out the rain.

Would I lay down my life a country to defend? I willingly would if it housed my friend.

It's thanks to your heart—as big and bold and blazing as the morning sun—that I rise each day knowing I am loved.

Your silent companion-ship is often more healing than words of advice.

A true friend likes you even when you don't like yourself. She will point out all your good qualities and convince you you're worthy of every good thing that happens to you.

If you listen to two good friends having a conversation, it sounds like two finely tuned musical instruments—they're in perfect pitch with one another.

You are there for me any time and for any reason.

Our friendship knows no hour or season.

A good friend makes you feel like the brightest star in the sky, the boldest color in a rainbow, the sweetest flower in a garden.

She finds the best in you and brings it out for everyone else to see.

Time spent with a true friend is nourishment for the soul.

In the presence of my best friend, I am nothing more or less than myself.

Sometimes the best medicine is a friend's voice on the phone.

I often wonder
what I could do
to repay someone
as nice as you.
I guess I can
only try to be
the kind of friend
you are to me.

A friend's smile leaves an imprint on your heart.

Friendship usually begins with two people discovering their similarities, but the relationship is firmly established when they learn to appreciate each other's differences.

A true friend knows when you want to talk...and when you don't.

*Friendship is
a special package—
to be handled with care,
to be gratefully
acknowledged,
and whose value we
should always esteem.*

If not for the wealth of my friendships, indeed, I would be poor.

The strongest friendships have experienced the joy of genuine forgiveness.

When I look around
at all the things that mean
the most to me,
   Your friendship means
a whole lot more than
anything I see.

I'd like a little
money.
I'd like a little ease.
But a friendship
that is faithful
Can outweigh both
of these.

Our closest friends challenge us to change, to grow, to become the best we can be.

A friend says
things to make you feel
smart.
A good friend makes you
feel strong.
A great friend tells when
you do things right.
A best friend tells you
when you're wrong.

*Friendship is
a flower that blooms
through all life's
seasons.*

Though we may be many miles apart, The ribbon of your friendship binds my heart.

We didn't exactly
see eye to eye
As our friendship teetered
and years rolled by.
But thanks to the fences
you'd always mend
I'm lucky today that
you call me friend.

*Friends like
you don't happen
along every day.
I'm glad you
happened to me.*

Friendships are like flowers—some last a few days, some last much longer.

The best ones will thrive if they're given tender loving care.

While polishing my memories, I discovered those shared with friends are among my most treasured keepsakes.

Friendships are the golden threads woven into the tapestry of our lives.

*O*nly God could
have given me a friend
as wonderful as you.
"Every good gift and
every perfect gift is from
above."

James 1:17

You are forever changed when you find a true friend.

ACKNOWLEDGMENTS

CONTRIBUTING WRITERS

Georgann Gouryeb-Freeman is a writer and graphic artist with a special interest in poetry.

Judy A. Hershner specializes in writing short, inspirational pieces for secular and religious audiences.

Katherine Q. Lyons is a widely published writer in the areas of human development and emotional well-being.

LeAnn Thieman is a motivational author and speaker whose message inspires audiences across the country.

Katheryne Lee Tirrell writes sentimental verses and poetry for the greeting card market.

PICTURE CREDITS

Front cover: **Elizabeth Mowry**

Elizabeth Mowry; SuperStock: Christie's Images, London; Gallery Contemporanea, Jacksonville; Private Collection/Helen Vaughn.